To the Tiger, Dog and Goat in my life
— I love you! EWN

To those who have more than one
place to call home. XL

Published in the UK by Scholastic, 2022
Scholastic, Bosworth Avenue, Warwick, CV34 6UQ
Scholastic Ireland, 89E Lagan Road, Dublin Industrial Estate, Glasnevin, Dublin, D11 HP5F

SCHOLASTIC and associated logos are trademarks and/or
registered trademarks of Scholastic Inc.

Text © Eva Wong Nava, 2022
Cover and inside illustrations © Xin Li, 2022

The moral rights of Eva Wong Nava and Xin Li have been asserted by them.

ISBN 978 0702 31573 2

A CIP catalogue record for this book is available from the British Library.

All rights reserved.
This book is sold subject to the condition that it shall not, by way of trade or otherwise, be lent, hired out or otherwise circulated in any form of binding or cover other than that in which it is published. No part of this publication may be reproduced, stored in a retrieval system, or transmitted in any form or by any other means (electronic, mechanical, photocopying, recording or otherwise) or used to train any artificial intelligence technologies without prior written permission of Scholastic Limited. Subject to EU law Scholastic Limited expressly reserves this work from the text and data mining exception.

Printed in China
Paper made from wood grown in sustainable forests and other controlled sources.

3 5 7 9 10 8 6 4 2

This is a work of fiction. Any resemblance to actual people, events or locales is entirely coincidental.

www.scholastic.co.uk

For safety or quality concerns:
UK: www.scholastic.co.uk/productinformation
EU: www.scholastic.ie/productinformation

# I LOVE CHINESE NEW YEAR

### EVA WONG NAVA AND XIN LI

**■SCHOLASTIC**

The Lunar New Year is arriving tomorrow!
A new moon. A new year. A new celebration.
My family is Chinese and we have our own
Lunar New Year traditions.

We start to clean the WHOLE house
a week before the new year.
I help Mama and Baba decorate,
making our home festive and cheerful.

For happiness, Mama
and I hang up a row of
red lanterns.

For health, Baba places
sticks of green bamboo
and pink cherry blossoms
around the house.

For good luck, Mama hangs a portrait with the word 'Fu' upside down.

And for good wishes, Baba and I put out dishes of eight tangerines.

Then, we wait for someone special to arrive for the most important dinner of the year.

# DIIIING DOOOONG!

My heart bursts with happiness to see Nai Nai at the front door. "Oh, my grandchild, you're taller than I can remember," she says, tousling my mop of waves.

"Come in, come in, our guest of honour," Baba says, giving his mother a wide smile and big hug.

"Welcome, welcome, our family is reunited again," Mama says, helping Nai Nai into the house.

We always have Reunion Dinner the night before Lunar New Year, with all sorts of special dishes. We celebrate by eating . . .

fish for lots of good luck . . .

a plate heaped with noodles for a long life . . .

dumplings for extra special blessings . . .

and a WHOLE chicken roasted to perfection!

"Here's the nian gao I made for this special occasion," Nai Nai says, offering me a slice.

"Higher and higher we climb to success for that's what nian gao means. Eat now, so I can begin my story for the evening."

I bite into my sticky dessert and wait for my grandma to start the story of the Great Race. It's a folktale of how the Lunar New Year began in China many, many moons ago.

"Twelve animals, one for each year, each one with their own special powers. It all started with a race to cross the most heavenly of rivers."

"What powers do I have?"

"Ah, my little Mai-Anne, you are Monkey – agile and intelligent."

"Rat was first. She's clever and imaginative. Second was Ox. He's strong and trustworthy. Tiger came third. Tiger is charming and popular. Fourth was Rabbit who is gentle and kind."

"Rabbit reminds me of your soft cuddles, Nai Nai."
"Come here and I'll give you a cuddle now, before I tell you what Dragon did."

"Dragon flew in at fifth. He's adventurous, flying around the world at high speed all the time."

"Snake s-s-s-lithered in sixth. Snake is creative and smart."

"Like Mama, who is good at art."
"You're so very right, just look at that lovely painting she made."

"Trot, trot, trot. Horse raced in at seventh. He's warm-hearted and energetic.

Goat took eighth place. He's friendly and steady."
"Just like Baba, who's always here for us."

"Your Baba is the best, Mai-Anne, you're a lucky one."

"Monkey you already know, so let's go to tenth place.

Rooster is hard working and is always on time.

At eleventh, it was Dog. She's faithful and helpful.

Finally, we have Pig. He is generous and good-tempered."

"Pig is like Uncle Eric, who always gives me a big hong bao on new year's day."

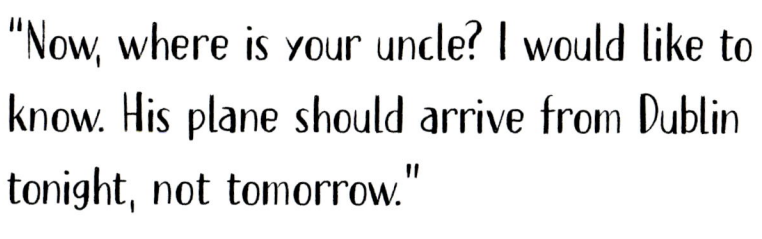

"Now, where is your uncle? I would like to know. His plane should arrive from Dublin tonight, not tomorrow."

# DIIIING DOOOONG!

"Here I am, everyone," Uncle Eric says, "and it looks like I'm just in time for our Family Dragon Dance."

Nai Nai gives him the **tightest hug.** I can tell she's happy to see her son at last.

Nai Nai begins to stoop, swing and swoop.
She's our very own mythical family Dragon,
flying around the room
with a fantastic fiery loop!

Uncle Eric holds a ball in his hand for Dragon Nai Nai to catch.
This is the pearl of wisdom and knowledge.

For supper, Nai Nai peels sweet tangerines and feeds me some pieces for good luck.

"Mai-Anne, here's a red dress I got you for the first day of the lunar year."

Red is for good luck, Nai Nai reminds me. I can't wait to put on my lucky new dress.

I love spending time with Nai Nai. She is adventurous and full of energy.

I love the Lunar New Year
because it's full of fun traditions.
I love being from a Chinese family –
there's no other way I would rather be.
Most of all, I love my Nai Nai and she loves me.

# Eight Lucky Facts about Chinese New Year

1. The lunar new year is also known as the Chinese New Year.

2. It begins on a new moon in January or February, and is celebrated for the first fifteen days by the Chinese worldwide.

3. The Chinese are not the only ones celebrating the lunar new year.

4. The Vietnamese new year falls on the same day as the Chinese New Year. They call it Tết, and it is celebrated for the first three days.

5. The word fú 福 is always hung upside down by the front door. 福 means 'wealth' in Mandarin. And when it is upside down, it means that Fortune has already stepped inside.

6. Mandarin oranges or tangerines are shared as symbols of good luck and prosperity. Each piece looks like an ingot, an ancient Chinese coin.

7. Red packets (hong bao) containing money are also exchanged for blessings and good wishes.

8. Eight is a lucky number.

### Five Fiery Facts about the Dragon Dance

1. In ancient China, the five-claw dragon was closely associated with the Emperors of China, who were known as Dragon Kings.

2. The Chinese dragon is a symbol of wisdom, harmony and peace.

3. The Dragon Dance is performed during the Lunar New Year by professionally trained martial arts experts.

4. The Dragon is an auspicious symbol. It stands for good luck and abundant blessings.

5. A Chinese dragon has folds in odd numbers: nine, eleven or thirteen. The Chinese believe these numbers stand for long life and prosperity.